BEYOND NEW ENGLAND THRESHOLDS

Haskell House

*Photographs and Comment
by*
SAMUEL CHAMBERLAIN

HASTINGS HOUSE   NEW YORK CITY

Concord Antiquarian Society

HOUSES ILLUSTRATED

Parson Capen House, Topsfield, Mass.
　　　　　　　　　　　　Half title, 1, 7, 27
John Balch House, Beverly, Mass. 8
Old Ironworks House, Saugus, Mass. 9
Whipple House, Ipswich, Mass. 6, 9-11
Tristram Coffin House, Newbury, Mass. . . 11, 12
Hyland House, Guilford, Conn. 13
Abraham Browne Jr. House, Watertown, Mass.
　　　　　　　　　　　Front end paper, 14-15
Haskell House, West Gloucester, Mass.
　　　　　　　　　　　　　Title Page, 16-19
House in Rockport, Mass. 20-22, 24
Linsley Homestead, Northford, Conn. . . . 23, 24
Ogden House, Fairfield, Conn. 25
Hathaway House, Salem, Mass. 26
John Ward House, Salem, Mass. . Frontispiece, 28
Lye Cobbler's Shop, Salem, Mass. 28
Longfellow's Wayside Inn . . Front Jacket, 29-32
House of the Concord Antiquarian Society,
　Concord, Mass. 4,5,32,33,34,39,40,69,76,80,81,92,93
House of Seven Gables, Salem, Mass. . . . 34-36
Pardee-Morris House, New Haven, Conn. . 37-39
House in Redding, Conn. 39, 82
Warner House, Portsmouth, N. H. 40-42
Royall House, Medford, Mass. 43-46

John Paul Jones House, Portsmouth, N. H. . . 46
Short House, Newbury, Mass. 47-48
Bubier House, Marblehead, Mass. 48
House in Marblehead, Mass. 48
Peter Jayne House, Marblehead, Mass. . . . 49, 54
Captain Trevitt House, Marblehead, Mass. . 50-51
Tobias Lear House, Portsmouth, N. H. . . . 52
King Hooper House, Marblehead, Mass. . . 53-54
Wentworth-Gardner House, Portsmouth, N. H. . 55-60
Richard Derby House, Salem, Mass. . . . 60-61
Moffatt-Ladd House, Portsmouth, N. H. . . 62-65
Lee Mansion, Marblehead, Mass. . . . 66, 68, 69
Sargent-Murray-Gilman-Hough House,
　Gloucester, Mass. 68, 69, 70
Wentworth Mansion, Portsmouth, N. H. . . 70-73
Peirce-Nichols House, Salem, Mass. 74-76
East India House, Salem, Mass. 77
Harrison Gray Otis House, Boston, Mass. . . 78-80
Cape Ann Historical House, Gloucester, Mass. . 81, 92
Dalton House, Newburyport, Mass. 82
Pingree House, Salem, Mass. 82-87
Winsor House, Duxbury, Mass. 87
Gore Place, Waltham, Mass. 88-91, 96
Samuel Fowler House, Danversport, Mass. . 94, 95

Copyright 1937 by
SAMUEL CHAMBERLAIN

PRINTED IN THE UNITED STATES OF AMERICA

THE JOHN WARD HOUSE (1684)   *Salem, Mass.*

BEYOND NEW ENGLAND THRESHOLDS

Concord Antiquarian Society

FOREWORD

AN old white house in the sun was taken as a symbol of rural New England in the first book of this series. Smiling and serene, framed in ancient elms, it personified many pleasant externals of this historic corner of America. But behind its sunny facade, across its inviting doorstep, there lies another symbol, more intimate and revealing, the hearth.

No more fitting theme could be found for the present volume, which is devoted entirely to early interiors, than the hearth. From the pioneer days, when newly arrived English carpenters built their Elizabethan manor houses around a huge central chimney stack bristling with fireplaces, until the time of McIntyre and Bulfinch, when the mantel became an exquisite plaything, the hearth was the sensitive barometer of New England life and progress. The first intrepid explorers lost no time in building themselves crude mud-and-plaster fireplaces, attaching rough shelters to this vital source of heat and cooking. The Colonial family clung close to the gigantic brick hearth in its kitchen living room during the exciting pioneer days of the 17th century. Under its broad lintel of hewn oak the good housewife kept pots stewing and spits turning. In its brick ovens she baked her corn bread and pudding and beans. On winter nights its roaring blaze warmed the whole family, huddled close in high-backed benches.

As the tension eased and prosperity rewarded the labor and ingenuity of early New Englanders, a more gracious and comfortable mode of living prevailed. Pure structural necessity gave way to a more academic viewpoint. The fireplace reflected this change, and became the central motif of a panelled wall, at first rather crude and unsymmetrical, but later finely balanced. Still the sole source of heat, the fireplace relinquished some of its utility as a cook stove. Pots and grills became rarer. Deep, well carved moldings, framing the fireplace opening, became more frequent. Responding to the artistic influence of the Renaissance, the panelled wall continued to develop refinements until after the Revolution. Then a new and delicate force began to be felt across the sea, that of the Brothers Adam. The day of the great shipping and merchant princes was at hand, and with it a scale of living which can be exemplified by the imposing mansions of Salem and Beacon Hill. Here the fireplace disengages itself from the woodwork, and becomes a cameo-like jewel set in the wall, enlivened by Dutch tiles, or perhaps by carvings from the inspired chisel of Samuel McIntyre.

As the symbolic hearth progressed from mud-and-stones to McIntyre, so did the entire house. So did the art of living and the whole institution of American taste and manners. It is the aspiration of these pages to sketch the story of this progress by means of the photographic image. No attempt has been made to cover so vast a subject completely. But its *essence* may be caught by a significant cross-section of typical examples quite as well as by exhaustive text and detail.

Some forty-five characteristic houses, therefore, have contributed to this intimate pictorial record of old

New England interiors. To the owners of these houses, who have offered every kindness and assistance, the author begs to express a very sincere gratitude. Many and varied are the architectural types found in this collection. There are late-Gothic, provincial manors which, with their overhangs, steep roofs and leaded casement windows, might have been transplanted direct from the English countryside. There are fortified garrison houses and "salt-box" farm-houses whose exterior lines are quite as satisfying as their inner charm. There are old, historic inns, and the homes of sea captains, handsomely panelled by ships' carpenters. The prosperous middle 18th Century brought in stately, academic residences with a pronounced feeling for symmetry, space and comfort. From this period several typical houses are shown. Finally, from the Adam-inspired Federal period, there are suave, patrician three-story mansions of merchant princes and wealthy sea captains, illustrated by the proud estates of Salem and Portsmouth. The impulse of the French Empire style is beginning to be felt in the last houses shown in the book, which ends well before the avalanche of bad taste that swept through most of the 19th century, not in America alone, but over Europe as well.

Some of these forty-five houses are of historical importance. Some are coupled with names famous in our history and literature. Others are entirely obscure and unheralded. Some speak of a grim struggle for existance; many reflect opulence and dignity. Each of them has a significant part in this pictorial pageant. The majority of the houses, incidentally, are open to the public at certain times of the year. Naturally many of the most outstanding examples were chosen for this volume, but it should be emphasized that abundant material of this same sort can be found throughout New England. This story could be told again in pictures, and charmingly, using 45 entirely different houses. The photographs have been arranged in chronological order, as far as possible, so as to portray the development which took place between the time of the Puritan pioneer and the opulent epoch of the early 19th century. Along with transitions in fireplaces and panelling, other interesting changes can be observed in the passing panorama of these photographs. There is the growth of the house plan, for example, from a primitive cluster of rooms clinging to one huge chimney, to a large, open, central-hall plan with ample space and circulation. There is the gradual enrichment of ornament from the first crude chamfering on "summer" beams to the elaborate carving on 19th century stair rails, cornices, doorways and mantels. The treatment of wall surfaces goes through many evolutions between early sheathing of hand-hewn pine and delicate picture paper imported from France. Ironwork and textiles show an equally pronounced transition. Old furniture, of course, affords a separate theme quite as important and engrossing as that of old houses. The ever changing influence of European styles on our early furniture is apparent in this chronology of pictures. More intangible, but most significant of all, is the gradual development of American character and tradition which took place before this intimate background. It is the very life of a young and courageous nation which is reflected in this graphic narrative.

Whipple House, Ipswich, Mass.

Parson Capen House (1683) Topsfield, Mass.

A nail-studded front door swings open and throws a flood of light upon the typical interior of a 17th Century New England house. A whole plan of living is revealed by this one swift view of a narrow hallway. The life of a pioneer household flows through it, upstairs and down, from kitchen to living room hearth. Let us cross the threshold, and from this vantage point explore a few of our earliest, and loveliest old houses.

At once we are face to face with fundamentals. The loom and the flax reel are decorative curiosities now, but they were vital necessities when John Balch came to America with his bride in 1626. This native of Somersetshire established a noble family tree, as the chart on the left will prove.

John Balch built the first part of his house in 1638. It was but one and a half stories high, and this was probably the upstairs bedroom. There is a sturdy beauty, but not a great deal of comfort, in the extremely low wooden bed.

John Balch House

*Old Ironworks House
Saugus, Mass.*

Life in those early days was centered about the hearth, principal source of warmth, nourishment and cheer. A battery of ingenious iron implements and a plentiful supply of blazing logs could produce a most acceptable family meal. The fireplace opening was often spanned by a mammoth lintel of hewn oak such as this.

*Whipple House (1638-40)
Ipswich, Mass.*

Side walls were usually finished in severe white plaster in these mediaeval examples, while the fireplace wall was faced with vertical pine boards, molded at the edges. The wood was left unpainted, to darken beautifully with age and smoke. Floors were scrubbed and sanded to smoothness.

The atmosphere of a convivial English taproom which prevails in the John Whipple house is enhanced by a cavernous fireplace and a magnificent beamed ceiling, one of the most massive and well constructed in New England. Its principal "summer" beams are long enough to cross each other, a structural rarity indeed.

Both the summer beam, and the sturdy post which supports it, are embellished with a restrained bit of carving, or "chamfering," evidence that the earliest builders paid some deference to beauty. The irregular wallboards provide a fitting background for old furniture of the period.

Whipple House

Whipple House — The silhouette of an old canopied bed transforms this severe and primitive bedroom into a thing of airy grace. Ipswich's most vitriolic pastor, the Reverend Whitefield, once lived in this house.

The fireplace of the Tristram Coffin House in Newbury has changed but little in the last two hundred years.

The upper hall of the Whipple House is stern in its simplicity. The house is now the home of the Ipswich Historical Society.

An old dresser for pewter, as handsome as it is handy, graces the combined living room and kitchen of this venerable house. This room is part of a wing which was added about 1693, after Tristram Coffin's earlier house (circa 1651) proved inadequate to shelter his rapidly increasing family.

Simple and most unconventional panelling replaces the vertical wood sheathing in this heartwarming fireplace wall. Cupboards are inserted above the lintel, and brick ovens are built into the chimney. It hardly seems necessary to add spinning wheels and brooms as further reminders of the industry of the pioneer housewife.

Tristram Coffin House

Hyland House (1660)
Guilford, Conn.

Built about 1660, the celebrated Hyland House was rebuilt in 1720. These dates explain the later and more sophisticated panelling in this room, but fail to account for the headlong pitch of the panelled partition or the impressive door frame given to the cupboard.

The antiquity of the Hyland House is more apparent in this utterly simple fireplace in one of the bedrooms, framed in the plainest of wall boards. A touch of startling grace is added by the andirons, whose design is as buoyant and gazelle-like as anything done by modern sculptors in metal.

Definitely of the later period, this mantel of the Hyland House is framed in a handsome rounded "bolection" molding. While it lacks the subtle proportions of later work, it is a superb example of the woodworker's craft.

A fireplace large enough to hold an entire family, without scorching its shins, is made possible by the span of this tremendous hand-hewn lintel. A coat of whitewash brightens up the brick opening of one of the most Gothic and Gargantuan of New England hearths.

Abraham Browne Jr. House (1663) Watertown, Mass.

Here is the conventional wall sheathing of flat white pine boards, but this time, to vary the monotony they are laid horizontally. They are oiled and waxed, and weathered a delicious toast brown. The floor boards are also of white pine, wide and durable, and the ceiling is a sturdy network of hewn oak beams.

Abraham Browne Jr. House

The bedroom of the Abraham Browne Jr. House has a hospitable hearth and a bright coat of whitewash. It must have been rather chill and cheerless in the middle of a New England winter, however. There were wide slits between the floorboards, and plenty of other places where the cold could steal in.

*Haskell House
(before 1652)
West Gloucester, Mass.*

This bedroom in the Haskell House, West Gloucester, Mass., has managed to keep its ancient wall boards and beamed ceiling, and still present an inviting interpretation of what we call modern comfort. The fine old highboy adds greatly to the picture.

A fascinating example of a 17th Century living room is found in the Haskell House. Vertical sheathing is carried over the fireplace lintel, and the battery of cooking utensils becomes truly formidable. It is not difficult to imagine a wizened bookkeeper of the 1660's bent over the high stretcher desk at the left.

Another wall of this room reveals a string of posnets hanging below the rafters, a ship model resting on an old spice box, and a primitive applique rug covering the wall above an old bible box. Relics of an adventurous 17th Century all, as are the large slat-back armchairs.

Haskell House

Old snowshoes and bear traps recall the rigors of those early winters. This house was built by Richard Window, the official joiner that came in the "Vanitie" with the first colony settlement, landing in 1627. In August 1652 he transferred his property to William Haskell, whose name has been given to the house ever since.

The walls and furniture of this ancient room make a symphony of satiny, lustrous browns and greys, weathered by the smoke of countless hearth fires.

Haskell House

Pewter played an important part in these pioneer households. Most of it came from England.

Haskell House

A close-up of this fireplace brings out a variety of tongs, skewers and brooms, and Jacobean and Queen Anne braziers, side by side.

Haskell House

Haskell House

The good housewife needed an imposing battery of kitchen utensils around her fire. There were tongs, trammels and toasters, skillets, skimmers and shovels, broilers, bellows and bed warmers. Not to mention the andirons, ladles, griddles, toddy sticks, and pipe lighters which do not lend themselves to the artifice of alliteration.

Smaller in scale, but equally inviting, is the unsymmetrical fireplace found in this old Rockport house. The fireplace seems dwarfed, partly because of the imposing dimensions of the old Carver armchair next to it. This panelling dates from 1780, though the house is a hundred years older.

House in Rockport, Mass. (circa 1680)

The early armchairs and tables were curiously oversized for the small, low-ceilinged rooms which they furnished. This building was originally the old "garrison house," fortified with an overhanging upper story on all four sides. It was probably built for the protection of woodcutters and fishermen against Indian raids.

House in Rockport.

House in Rockport. The dining room is embellished by an ancient and well filled cupboard.

House in Rockport. A glimpse of the Southeast living room.

House in Rockport, Mass. The north wing dining room was added to this Rockport house in 1778, a fact which is revealed at once by the fireplace wall. The light Carver side chairs, the table, and the chandelier belong to the earlier period.

This old house in Rockport is supposed to have served as a refuge for Elizabeth Proctor, who, with her husband, was convicted of witchcraft in Salem in 1692. Her husband was hanged, but Elizabeth escaped a similar fate on condition that she leave Salem forever.

The north bedroom of this old Rockport house dates from 1778. Its mantel, built well into the room, is similar to many others on Cape Ann, but its painted window shades are rare indeed.

Linsley Homestead (1680) Northford, Conn.

A glimpse into one of the oldest dining rooms in Connecticut reveals a crude corner cupboard brightening up the pine board walls, and some Fiddle-back chairs silhouetted against the light. The length of exposure of this photograph may be guessed by the blurred hands on the clock.

The old kitchen of the Linsley Homestead has gradually changed complexion until it assumes the character of a very comfortable living room. The ample fireplace is but one of three on the ground floor which are built into an overwhelming stone chimney stack.

An early pine cupboard shimmers against the dark sheathing of the dining room in the Linsley Homestead.

Corner of the West bedroom in the Rockport house.

Ogden House
Fairfield, Conn.

Stone chimney pieces and massive oak lintels were the rule, rather than the exception in early Connecticut houses. This rustic kitchen was built in the lean-to of an old "salt-box" farmhouse. Note the rough hewn beams and the array of wooden plates.

Ogden House

If crudity still reigned in the kitchen, a degree of refinement was creeping into the dining room. Witness the dignified panelling encasing the fireplace. The wall remained austerely white, an effective background for a bannister-back armchair.

The importance of the kitchen living room in the life of pioneer New Englanders is well illustrated in the Hathaway House, where a loom, a highboy, a gate-leg table and several slat-back side chairs crowd in on the culinary department.

Hathaway House (1682) Salem, Mass.

The kitchen fireplace, built of rough, uneven bricks, is shallow and business-like. This house was formerly Salem's oldest bakery. It preserves the authentic stamp of an Elizabethan Gothic manor as well as any house in America.

Hathaway House

The Parson Capen House is another near-perfect relic of the 17th Century. Its primitive kitchen has the almost uncanny appearance of being left undisturbed for the last 250 years. Wood completely dominates this room. Walls, floors, ceiling, furniture, utensils, containers, even dishes, are made of it.

Parson Capen House

The "parlor," even in pioneer days, was a relatively unused room, given over to "retirement" and the entertainment of special guests. The slat-back Carver armchairs and the gate-leg table are contemporary with the house, whose date is inscribed on a summer beam as "JULY Ye 8th 1683."

In the lean-to of the John Ward House in Salem is installed a fascinating old "cent shop," preserving a flawless picture of a small village store in Colonial days. The glass case contains a toothsome assortment of cookies, candies and trinkets which delighted your great-great-grandmother as a child.

(1684)

Nearby is a cobbler's shop, preserved exactly as it was a century or so ago, including a classic poster advertising "Dr. Pierce's Family Medicines." This shop and the John Ward House have been perpetuated by the Essex Institute.

Lye Cobbler's Shop, Salem, Mass.

One of the most visited buildings in New England is the venerable hostelry made famous by Longfellow's "Tales of a Wayside Inn." Built in 1686 by Samuel Howe, it was run as a tavern by five generations of genial Howe landlords. Save for a period between 1860 and 1896 it has always been maintained as an inn. Many additions were made to the original structure, one of the most unique being the ballroom, whose atmosphere of discreet conviviality may perhaps be transmitted by this view.

The low-vaulted ballroom of the Wayside Inn has a floor of plain boards, surrounded by hard wall benches, inside of which the guests stored their wraps. Three eight-candle chandeliers furnished the illumination on quadrille night, and two fireplaces supplied the heat. The orchestra enjoyed a chaste raised platform.

Definitely of the pioneer days is the old dining room of the Inn, where guests sat at a rustic table and saw their fowl roasted on the kitchen spit. A favored spot on winter evenings was the old wooden bench close to the fire. Its high back reached to the floor, preventing chill backdrafts.

Less robust, and somewhat more restful, is the parlor of the Wayside Inn, panelled in the manner of the early 18th Century. Over the mantel is the Howe coat-of-arms, flanked by the two panes of glass "writ on near a century ago by the great Major Molineaux."

A number of original Howe furnishings of the Wayside Inn have been brought back to give the old bedrooms their original appearanace. A handsome mantel, a Windsor combback chair and a superb canopied bed help to make this a most noteworthy room.

Rooms in the Wayside Inn are named after some of its distinguished guests: Washington, Lafayette, Longfellow, Edison. This bedroom boasts a trundle bed which slips out from under the old four poster, and thus doubles the sleeping accommodations.

A graphic picture of what a 17th Century room looked like when *new* is provided by this reproduction of a typical New England kitchen living room in the late Gothic tradition. The leaded casement windows, the chamfered beam ceiling and the very romantic furniture all are reminiscent of the provincial manor houses in England.

House of the Concord Antiquarian Society, Concord, Mass.

One of the rarities of the house of the Concord Antiquarian Society is a heavy American oak press cupboard, originally used to store provisions.

This vista into the 17th Century room reveals the Spanish and Flemish influence which was strangely manifest in the finer furniture of the time.

The kitchen fireplace in this room of the Concord Antiquarian Society's House is built of large, uneven bricks, framed in a pine molding. Besides the housewife's utensils, there is a pipe box for the man of the house, and some ember tongs to light his tobacco.

One of the very few survivors among entirely pine-sheathed rooms is found in the house of the Concord Antiquarian Society. The pine ceiling is a decided rarity, and comes from the first half of the 18th century, as do the pine chest, gate-leg table and low country slat-back chairs.

The venerable Turner-Ingersoll House in Salem, built in 1668, presents a pure Elizabethan exterior. Inside, however, it bears the stamp of several later periods, as this hallway proves. It became known as the "House of Seven Gables" after the publication of Hawthorne's great romance.

Some very handsome panelling was built into the living room of the House of Seven Gables in 1720. Flanking the fireplace are two pilastered motifs, one of which contains a china closet with a well-carved shell top. In it are displayed, among other things, a Bristol bowl, some French wine glasses, a Liverpool pitcher, much pink lustre ware and a Lowestoft tea service, in addition to more lowly ginger jars, tea cannisters and pickle bottles. The portrait over the mantel is of Mary Turner, descendant of the builder, who later became Mrs. Daniel Sargent. A Duncan Phyfe table graces the center of the room. The house contains a secret staircase, possibly built against a recurrence of Salem's witchcraft persecution.

Besides a Hepplewhite sideboard and a Willard clock, the dining room of the House of Seven Gables contains a dinner wagon and tray which belonged to Susan Ingersoll, Hawthorne's morose spinster cousin, who lived in the house. Hawthorne was one of the few visitors allowed beyond the threshold.

The great chamber, or "Phoebe's room," on the second floor, is distinguished by a Sheraton four-poster, a Queen Anne highboy and table, and an old Salem chest, besides the august portrait of that eminent mathematician, Nathaniel Bowditch.

The House of Seven Gables

Among the abandoned spinning wheels in the attic of the House of Seven Gables is a fragment of the original 1668 door, and a miniature model of the house.

The old shop window in the House of Seven Gables glitters with souvenirs reminiscent of other centuries.

New Haven, Conn. The robust kitchen of the Pardee-Morris House is spanned by a magnificent ceiling of hewn oak beams, blackened by generations of smoke, and on one occasion, by flames. The house was looted and set afire by a party of Red Coats in 1779, but the structure was so solid that the flames were soon extinguished.

Pardee-Morris House Panelling makes a hesitant appearance in this cheerful room, finished in natural wood. The fireplace is but one of eight which are built into the two massive stone ends of this house, which is perhaps the outstanding example of this type of construction in New England.

Little remains of the original heart of the house, built in the 1680's. In its stead are quiet, unostentatious rooms, which reflect the simplicity and good taste of Yankee landowners in Revolutionary days. Early rugs, it will be noted, were used on the table as well as on the floor.

Pardee-Morris House

The atmosphere of a country "front room" pervades this corner of the house, aided by a prim mantel, an old-fashioned spinnet and a Fiddle-back chair. The picture on the wall recalls the fact that another portrait in the house, that of Amos Morris, shows saber cuts made by British officers.

Pardee-Morris House

Natural wood finish lends itself well to corner cupboards, a fact which is proven by this shining example in the Pardee-Morris House.

Many Connecticut fireplaces are built of stone, but not many enjoy a shimmering coat of whitewash, or such a diversified array of old accessories. In Redding, Conn.

The Green Room in the Concord Antiquarian Society's remarkable house shows the irregular panelling and fluted pilasters which are so typical of the early 18th Century. There is an increasing refinement in the gate-leg table and the bannister-back chairs with carved crestings.

The Queen Anne Room in the house of the Concord Antiquarian Society begins to reflect the more formal mode of living which prevailed as the 18th century progressed. The fireplace wall has become symmetrical and well studied. The furniture shows the New England version of the Queen Anne style.

On a grand and unprecedented scale indeed was the mansion built in Portsmouth, N. H., by Captain Archibald Macphaedris in 1718, said to have cost 6,000 pounds. Its eighteen-inch thick walls were built of brick imported from Holland. Dutch tiles also frame its dining room fireplace.

The Macphaedris House, later known as the Warner House, was spacious on an almost regal scale. The impressive parlor was panelled from floor to ceiling, and the corner fireplace enjoyed a triple band of Dutch tiles. The portrait of the dainty young lady, Miss Polly Warner, was painted by Blackburn.

A doorway of the Warner House, viewed from the hall and from the imposing bedroom.

The great bed chamber on the second floor was also panelled to the ceiling. After more than two hundred years the panelling, and the house in general, are in almost flawless condition. Five years were needed to build it, but it was built to last! There are many fine Chippendale and Sheraton pieces in the house, and much of Captain Macphaedris's own furniture still remains. The view directly above shows the mural painting in the hall, supposedly the work of Langdon Towne, the hero of "Northwest Passage."

Warner House

Another patrician estate of the time was the Royall House in Medford, Mass., built in 1732 around the remains of an old farmhouse. The central hall makes an impressive appearance here, allowing room for an elaborate carved stairway and a passageway directly through the house.

Royall House — Colonel Isaac Royall had definite ideas of grandeur, as the architecture of his mansion would seem to prove. Inside and out, it is a masterpiece of fine carving and carpentry. In its large, formal rooms, Colonel Royall entertained with lavish hospitality.

The living room of the Royall House is an ambitious bit of woodwork, embracing an arched recess on either side of the fireplace, and a handsomely carved pilaster treatment. The fireplace enjoys an abundance of Dutch tiles.

The grace of Chippendale furniture is in keeping with the sensitive proportions of these old rooms. Fine furniture, however, was but one of Colonel Royall's possessions. When his house was finished, his wife moved up from Antigua, their West Indies home, bringing twenty-seven slaves with her. The brick building which was built to shelter the slaves is still standing, one of the few of its kind in New England. During the Revolution the mansion served as headquarters for Stark's Division at the time of the Siege of Boston.

Royall House

Royall House   The motif of a fireplace flanked by two arched recesses is also carried out, this time with Corinthian pilasters, in an impressive bedroom on the second floor. A broken molding makes its appearance around the fireplace opening. The space above it is filled by a very wide, single panel.

The Royall House has three ample stories, built between two massive ends of brick, each of which contains two chimneys and a nest of fireplaces. Almost every room in the house has its grate, but it is doubtful if they were sufficient to make the house comfortable in the middle of winter.

The kitchen fireplace in the Royall House must have been the scene of flurried activity during one of the Colonel's large dinner parties. This fireplace has a very deep oven and an efficient battery of kettles. The two firemen's buckets, hanging from the mantel shelf, are a later and more sentimental touch.

This unaffected Colonial dining room is found in a Portsmouth house built by the well known merchant, Captain Purcell. After his death, his widow ran it as a boarding house, her prize lodger being Captain John Paul Jones, who was supervising the construction of the "Ranger" in 1777.

Short House (1733), Newbury, Mass. The panelling of this low-ceilinged parlor is unexpectedly enlivened by a china closet, an unsymmetrical touch which helps make a most charming room. Paint has been removed from the early pilasters and panelling, revealing wood of a beautiful, golden brown color.

Short House The upstairs bedroom of this house is more severe and symmetrical. This is also a "brick-end" house. The fireplace side of the room is panelled in weathered pine, while the other three walls are plastered. The wide floor boards are in superb condition.

Sunshine filters through the 24-paned windows of the Short House, emphasizing the unusual width of the muntins.

Typical of many an old sea captain's home is the Bubier House in Marblehead (c. 1720) whose cheerful interior is accented by a wag-on-the-wall clock.

The ceiling of this hospitable room proved to be too low for comfort, so the floor was lowered, creating the unusual effect of a raised fireplace. The elevated hearth makes an excellent fireside seat when the flames have subsided to embers.

Marblehead, Mass.

The salty atmosphere of clipper ships pervades the kitchen hearth of the old Peter Jayne House in Marblehead, built in 1724. The house was later owned by a member of Governor Hancock's staff, and was used for secret meetings of the Committee of Safety.

Peter Jayne House, Marblehead, Mass. Another view of the same room shows that the old kitchen has been converted into a dining room, with Windsor chairs surrounding the gate-leg table. This house is supposed to be one of the earliest Masonic meeting places in the country.

The doors and frames of many an old Marblehead house slope down at the end of the room. The Captain Trevitt House illustrates this vagary, which makes a choice bone of contention among architects. Some say that it was intentional; others contend that the supports of the house have sunk.

Many a Marblehead house was panelled by a ship's carpenter, who might be excused for bending a few corners to make his rooms resemble ships' cabins. This is a fair assumption, since Marblehead's rocky base hardly encourages a house to settle.

Captain Trevitt House, Marblehead, Mass.

The stair rail, which afforded the Colonial wood workers their most exuberant outbursts, is a joy forever to photographers. Few architectural details are more photogenic. Captain Trevitt, owner of this house, commanded an artillery company in the Battle of Bunker Hill.

One of the very early examples of a central hallway is found in the Tobias Lear House, built in Portsmouth, N.H., about 1740. It is brightened by a wooden floor painted in black-and-white "marble" squares. The wall paper is a Revolutionary pattern discovered on old fragments in the house.

George Washington sat before this fireplace in 1789 when he visited the home of Tobias Lear, the brilliant young man who became his private secretary upon graduating from Harvard. For a period of fourteen years Lear resided almost continually with the Washington family, and became a close confidant.

King Hooper House (1745), Marblehead, Mass. Robert Hooper, one of the wealthiest merchants in New England, entertained dignitaries from far and wide in the banquet hall of his Marblehead mansion. Two fireplaces furnished the heat for the long, half-vaulted room, and a graceful chandelier provided illumination.

So powerful did Robert Hooper become in the community, and so princely was his scale of living, that he was nicknamed "King" Hooper, a name which has clung to his houses. The hallway is embellished with a superb stairway, whose newel post is a masterpiece of intricate carving.

A closer view of the stairway in the King Hooper House shows three balusters, each turned with a different type of spiral, on each step. This plan gave a richness which was widely copied in later New England mansions. Note the deep-set panelling at the end of each stair.

The spaciousness and dignity of this cheerful bedroom is enhanced by a magnificent Queen Anne highboy and a Sheraton bed, whose graceful post appears in the foreground. There is a touch of the unusual in the panelling of the fireplace, which extends to the ceiling quite alone.

Peter Jayne House

The central hall plan, which provided ample circulation and two side chimneys instead of a narrow hallway and one large central chimney stack, probably reached the peak of achievement in the superb hallways of the Wentworth-Gardner House, built in Portsmouth in 1760. That a more gracious and dignified mode of living resulted is well demonstrated by this remarkable house.

The wood worker who carved this amazing mantel must have been seized by a mood of incorrigible and delightful fantasy, otherwise he never could have achieved so drastic and unfettered a release from the conventional forms. The Dutch tiles add to the general gaiety.

Wentworth-Gardner House

The grace and balance of the panelling in this room is equalled elsewhere throughout the Wentworth-Gardner House. Without doubt it is one of the finest examples of interior finish in New England, and it is not surprising that the Metropolitan Museum of Art acquired it some years ago.

The walls of the dining room were enriched with an old English paper when the house was in private hands, shortly before its sale to the Metropolitan.

Reflected in the delicate frame of an 18th century mirror is another glimpse of the ornate mantel in the Wentworth-Gardner House.

An old hurricane glass has the practical value of protecting a candle flame from the draft, and the decorative value of catching shining highlights.

The sepia-black of the old paper makes a fine foil for the white of the woodwork in this dining room, whose corner cupboard is a superb bit of carving. The patrician character of the old Portsmouth of pre-Revolutionary days is accurately reflected in this airy room.

Wentworth-Gardner House

The gentle art of dining becomes a more serene and satisfying ceremony, it would seem, when it occurs within walls as soothing and decorative as these.

Wentworth-Gardner House

The lower hallway of the Wentworth-Gardner House is distinguished enough, but the upper hall, shown in these two views, can lay claim to being the finest thing of its kind in this country. Note the rich cornice treatment around the landing window, and the extraordinary height of the balusters.

Seen from another angle, the upper hall reveals a formal architectural treatment, embracing deep-cut panels and dignified Ionic pilasters. The austere highboy lends a last note of formality. This hallway faces out on the broad surface of Portsmouth Harbor.

Few decorative innovations were as enthusiastically received in the Colonies as the Dutch tile. Painted by hand, in designs as original as they were amusing, they provided a touch of whimsy which brightened the formal hearths of that day.

Wentworth-Gardner House

One of the finest examples of pre-Revolutionary woodwork is found in the brick house which Captain Richard Derby erected at the head of famed Derby Wharf, in Salem. The panelling, which is accented with fine, deep-cut moldings, is painted an elusive shade of olive green.

(1762)

Richard Derby House — Something about this old room recreates the atmosphere of early Colonial days far more eloquently than mere words. The noble windows contribute a great deal to the effect. They are set deeply enough in the walls to provide window seats, and their panelled shutters are masterpieces of fine carpentry. In addition to olive green, the rooms in this house were painted in lustrous variations of grey-blue and maroon.

Unparalleled in New England are the spacious hall and almost regal stairway of the Moffatt-Ladd House in Portsmouth, N. H. Built in 1763 by Captain John Moffatt for his son Samuel, about to be married, the house is said to be a copy of Captain Moffatt's boyhood home in Hertfordshire.

The eye is struck at once by the richly ornamented soffit of the stairs, and by the rare and exquisite wall paper. This is the "Vues d'Italie" set, printed in Paris and better known as the bay of Naples paper. A Chippendale sofa lends the final touch to this beautiful handling of a difficult corner.

Moffatt-Ladd House

Moffatt-Ladd House Portsmouth was a prosperous, patrician, isolated Tory community in the middle-18th century, a fact which seems to be symbolized in this proud stairway. Even Grinling Gibbons himself is supposed to have done some of the carving for this extraordinary house.

Another view of the hall shows the bright harmony created by the handsome cutting of the wainscoat and door panels, the Bay of Naples paper, and the carved Flemish chairs. The front door, open at the left, once led to a majestic bluff overlooking the Piscataqua River.

Moffatt-Ladd House

This celebrated wall paper, which is also used on the upper hall, was printed by Joseph Dufour in Paris about 1815. It illustrates, among other subjects, the Bay of Naples, Tivoli, Amalfi and Vesuvius in eruption. The high balusters of the stair rail are alternately turned, twisted and fluted.

The dining room of the Moffatt-Ladd House is distinguished by a graceful wall paper pattern and a highly decorative niche, which affords protection to the sideboard.

One of the most luxurious mansions of Colonial days was built in 1768 by Colonel Jeremiah Lee, of Marblehead. The impressive state chamber is still decorated with the original wall paper which was painted for it in England. Two of Colonel Lee's Chippendale chairs remain in the corner.

The kitchen of the Lee Mansion has lost the utilitarian aspect which it had in the days of the Colonel's banquets, but it has gained a charming miscellany of china, spinning wheels, cradles, "chicken coop" Windsor chairs and a Queen Anne table.

Colonel Jeremiah Lee amazed the townsfolk with the grandiose scale of his house, whose original cost was ten thousand pounds. Besides the English wall paper, the interior woodwork was executed in England and shipped to Marblehead on the Colonel's own boats. The noble hall and stairway of the house are unique in American Colonial architecture. This view of the State Chamber shows the two Hepplewhite chairs which, according to tradition, belonged to Governor Hancock, and were later brought to Marblehead on a schooner. These two chairs were found, together with many other fine antique pieces, in the tottering hovel of two Marblehead characters, "Liz" and "Mopy" Chambers, when the authorities sent them to the poor house.

The work of Grinling Gibbons has a direct influence on the detail of this mantel in the Lee Mansion.

Washington, Jefferson, Lafayette and Andrew Jackson were entertained in this dining room of the Lee Mansion.

In Gloucester the same year, 1768, Winthrop Sargent was building a fine house as a wedding present for his daughter Judith, who married the founder of Universalism, John Murray. It is now known as the Sargent-Murray-Gilman-Hough House. This view shows the superb woodwork of one of the bedrooms.

The parlor mantel in the Sargent-Murray-Gilman-Hough House is architecturally ambitious.

The elaborate woodwork in this living room of the Lee Mansion was carved in natural English pine.

The Revolutionary bedroom in the house of the Concord Antiquarian Society contains a sensitive and informal bit of panelling, accented by two pilasters, and painted a gray-blue. The block-front high chest seen on the left was made to furnish the Old Manse, home of the militant Reverend William Emerson, the grandfather of the philosopher.

A superb white-painted stairway is found in the Sargent-Murray-Gilman-Hough House, its beauty enhanced by an unusually elaborate window on the staircase landing.

Governor Benning Wentworth, of New Hampshire, built one of New England's most remarkable (1750), rooms in his mansion at Little Harbor, near Portsmouth. It was the Governor's Council Chamber, dominated by a colossal, heavily carved chimney piece, a detail of which is shown in this view.

Reflected in the convex glass of an old girandole mirror, the sumptuous lines of the Council Chamber are distorted, but still impressive. Regular meetings of the Council were held here for several years. The guns of the Governor's Guard were racked in the adjacent hallway, and are still there.

There is dignity and great comfort in this bedroom of the Governor Wentworth Mansion. The bold wall paper pattern is the original design. The Governor may well have anticipated trouble in the Colonies, for he was careful to build a secret passageway in his house, for use in emergencies.

Governor Wentworth died in 1770, however, five years before the Revolution. This view shows the same room as above, seen from under the canopy of the bed. An early Franklin stove appears in front of the fireplace opening.

Governor Wentworth Mansion

This living room, with its fireplace retreating into a bevelled corner, was but one of a vast number of rooms (some accounts place them at fifty), which comprised the rambling, many-winged Wentworth Mansion. Underneath it was a huge cellar, capable of housing a fair sized cavalry troop.

An exposed rafter and a mantel shelf of debatable fitness lend variety to this most friendly room in the Wentworth Mansion. Governor Wentworth married his housemaid, Martha Hilton, who later became the heroine of Longfellow's poem, "Lady Wentworth."

Samuel McIntyre, the great carver-architect of Salem, enters the picture with the appearance of the Peirce-Nichols House, certainly one of the noblest three-story houses in New England. The exquisite beauty of the interior woodwork, well exemplified by this mantel detail, is unsurpassed in America.

(1782),

Photography has difficulty in capturing the fine subtleties of McIntyre's white-painted rooms. This bed chamber is one of his finest. Aided by his son, McIntyre spent many years working on the details of this house, which is frequently referred to as his masterpiece.

Peirce-Nichols House

The mantel in the East parlor of the Peirce-Nichols House dates from 1801, and reveals McIntyre's soundness as a designer as well as his mastery of carving. The old Empire mirror plays an important part in the design. McIntyre was born in 1757, the son of a joiner, and mastered the wood carver's craft as a youth. He stayed close to Salem all his life, never going abroad, and died there in 1811.

Two views of the central hallway of the Peirce-Nichols House, the second one seen from the East parlor.

The Chippendale room of the house of the Concord Antiquarian Society has Salem connections, since its panelling comes from the Captain Billy Cook House in that city. An atmosphere of restrained elegance pervades this hearthside, quite in keeping with the unruffled prosperity of that time.

One of McIntyre's first commissions was the execution of new woodwork for the East India House in Salem, (built 1706), where two of his mantels are to be found.

The convivial, stein-and-musket air of this room in the East India House recalls the fact that it has served as an inn, as well as one of the largest of Salem's early residences. During his American trip in 1824 Lafayette was entertained at a quadrille given in this house.

The dignity of Boston houses in the last years of the 18th century is well exemplified in the celebrated Harrison Gray Otis House, whose dining room bears such a strong Empire savor. There is documentary evidence that the old sideboard belonged to Paul Revere. *(1795), Boston, Mass.*

The luxurious dining room mantel in the Harrison Gray Otis House is surmounted by a portrait by John Greenwood. The identity of the subject is unknown.

A pitcher and bowl, as decorative as they are useful, appear in the rear bedroom of the same house.

The Harrison Gray Otis House is celebrated, among other things, for its exquisite mantels. This one in the front chamber has the American eagle for its central motif. The house is generally attributed to Charles Bulfinch, and is used at present as the headquarters of the Society for the Preservation of New England Antiquities.

A safe is concealed over the mantel in the office of the Otis House.

A mantel in the withdrawing room of the Otis House.

The reeded bedroom in the house of the Concord Antiquarian Society belongs to the period of 1800. The corner cupboard is much earlier in date. The two Chippendale chairs are the work of Joseph Hosmer, Concord's patriotic cabinet maker, who was a Lieutenant of the Minute Men.

The fireplace in the reeded room of the Concord Antiquarian Society's House.

This stairway in the same house contains five original posts from John Hancock's Beacon Hill mansion.

Cape Ann Historical House, Gloucester, Mass.

The bedroom of a Gloucester sea captain might have looked very much like this in the early days of the 19th century.

A noble staircase is found in the Dalton House, Newburyport, Mass.

Front doors divided in the Dutch manner are rare in New England. This one is in Redding, Conn.

An impeccable mantel in the Pingree House might well be taken as a symbol of the commercial prosperity, combined with extraordinary good taste, which dominated the life of Salem in the great merchant years of the early 19th century.

Pingree House (1804), Salem, Mass.

The Pingree House is McIntyre at his sensitive best, at the peak of his career, surely the finest brick house he ever built. There is a story behind the Venetian mirror which hangs in the hallway. It was found in the effects of a British soldier after the Evacuation, and was sold on Boston Common.

One of McIntyre's most graceful doors makes a frame for its companion in the Pingree House.

The stair rail of the Pingree House is in the Chippendale tradition.

A McIntyre mantel, a few exquisite pieces of Lowestoft, and the fragment of an old marine painting, these comprise a still-life which is eloquent of Salem at the peak of her maritime glory, when fortunes were made by her intrepid young captains in the China trade, and later spent upon sumptuous houses.

Pingree House

The wheat sheaf was one of McIntyre's favorite decorative motifs, a fact which is strikingly evident in the Pingree House. This detail of a mantel in the front parlor shows his carving at the summit of its perfection, even though his architecture may err slightly on the over-elaborate side.

The East front chamber of the Pingree House has recently been restored to its full dignity. The apricot and blue taffeta curtains, the Venetian blinds, the Sheraton work table and the chaise-longue all contribute to its authenticity. Over the mantel is a painting of "The Launching of the Fane."

A large Duncan Phyfe table and a set of Sheraton chairs distinguish the dining room of the Pingree House. The portrait is of Timothy Fitch, Boston merchant.

A restrained elegance marks the furniture and mantel in the West front chamber of the Pingree House.

There is a lyric quality to the hearthside of this rear bedroom in the Pingree House. An old armchair, covered with a decorative bedspread of the 1800's, and a highly pictorial fire screen both contribute to its subtle and sophisticated balance. Two Delft drug jars accentuate the grace of the mantel.

A mantel and cupboard have been effectively combined in the dining room of the old Winsor House, Duxbury, Mass.

The simple, scrupulously carved woodwork of the early 19th century lends itself well to this chaste and sunny boudoir in the Winsor House.

The New England house reached its most imposing scale in the mansion which Governor Christopher Gore erected in Waltham, Mass., in 1804. In its state reception hall were entertained the great men of the day, among them Lafayette, Tallyrand, Adams, Monroe and Daniel Webster.

A canopied bed seems to achieve its true distinction when placed in a high ceilinged room. This is one of the four masters' bedrooms in Gore Place. For the convenience of the occupants of these four rooms, twenty-two other rooms were built into this vast estate.

Across the shimmering silver and crystal of the reception hall table is a vista into the Oval Room, whose grandiose proportions at once recall the salons of Europe. Note that the tops of the lofty door frames follow the gentle bow of the oval rooms. The architect of Gore Place has never been identified, though Charles Bullfinch has often been mentioned.

The influence of the Brothers Adam is very strong in this mantel in the state reception room of Gore Place.

A subtly concave mantel and an abruptly convex girandole mirror combine gracefully in the Oval Room of Gore Place.

Under the roof of one of the low wings in Gore Place is a nursery, with child-high windows and a flat vaulted ceiling, furnished with a fine collection of early American children's pieces.

The visitor to Gore Place is confronted with a majestic circular sweep of stairs as soon as he enters the front hall. Various vicissitudes have befallen this noble house, and only recently it was in danger of being torn down and having its broad acres turned into building lots. It was rescued, however, by a group of appreciative citizens, who are now carrying on the work of restoring and furnishing it.

The McIntyre Room in the house of the Concord Antiquarian Society, while not actually the work of the Salem master, is in his individual style. The wall paper is a copy of a French Directoire design, and soft blue French brocade covers the chair cushions. The piano dates from about 1804.

The American eagle, that immensely popular post-Revolutionary symbol, flourished on much of the woodwork of that period. This is from the McIntyre Room above.

The fireplace and chimney were often built into the room in this period, thus preserving an unbroken exterior wall. From the Cape Ann Historical House.

The mantel of the McIntyre Room is strongly Adamesque in feeling. It was found in a house in Roxbury, Mass. which was occupied at one time by John Singleton Copley. The delicate fire screen and the steeple-top andirons are in the same sensitive scale.

The entrance hall of the house of the Concord Antiquarian Society is enriched by a copy of Georgian wall paper and by a staircase modelled after one which existed in the famous Hancock House on Beacon Hill.

There is a decided primness to the simple white woodwork and restrained furniture of this front parlor in the Fowler House, in Danversport, Mass. One of the best square, hip-roofed brick houses, it is a monument to the fine standards of construction prevalent around 1810.

Another parlor of the Fowler House is brightened by a decorative paper known as the "Roman Chase," printed from old blocks.

A detail of this mantel in the Fowler House reveals the subtle reeding in the woodwork, and the fine depth of the Roman Chase paper.

One of the glories of the Fowler House is its original wall paper, gay with festoons and medallions. The house and the wall paper both date from 1810, an epoch perilously close to the brink of bad taste. Nevertheless, they give no intimation of the sad decline which marked most of the 19th century. This, therefore, would seem to be an excellent place to bring these illustrations to an end.